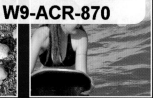

AMELIA ISLAND | A VISUAL ECSTASY

TABLE OF CONTENTS

PHOTOGRAPHS AND TEXT

Elizabeth G. Wilkes and
Elizabeth Wilkes Photography
904-206-2203
www.elizabethwilkesphotography.com

DESIGN AND PRINTING BY

Kelly R. Dodson
Sumter Printing Company
1295 Wilson Hall Rd.
Sumter, South Carolina
803-905-4444
www.sumterprinting.com

High aerial of Amelia Island from the north on Cumberland Sound.

Amelia Island is a delightful place to live and a great destination for vacations. This area has a very colorful history dating from more than 2000 years ago and Fernandina is the only town in the U.S.A. that has flown 8 different flags. The Amelia Island Historical Museum and several of the state parks have displays that clearly describe the diversity and changes over time in this area. Amelia is the most northern barrier island in eastern Florida. To the east is the Atlantic Ocean, to the north is Cumberland Sound and Cumberland Island and to the west is the Amelia River, a part of the Intra-coastal Waterway and the Florida mainland. To the south are several state parks and the city of Jacksonville, Florida.

High aerial of Amelia Island from the south on Nassau River.

There is always a majestic view on Amelia Island, from the marsh land to sunrises on the Atlantic Ocean.

(Top) The Shave Bridge looking north towards Fernandina. (Left) The Shave Bridge looking east. (Above) Fernandina Beach Municipal Airport.

Approaching Amelia Island from the mainland, highway A1A goes on the Shave Bridge over the Intra-coastal Waterway and the Amelia River and gives a first view of the Atlantic Ocean. To the south is the Fernandina Beach Municipal Airport where many small and large airplanes land and take off every day. On the left is the Amelia Island Yacht Basin, one of the several marinas on the island. Also the 2 paper mills and the Fernandina Beach Marina are visible. The town of Fernandina and Centre Street are tucked into a safe place on the Amelia River between them.

The Timucuan Indians lived in the area for many centuries and thrived on corn, beans, pumpkins, squash, fish, oysters and shellfish. They called their island Napoyea.

In 1562 the French were the first to raise their flag, followed by the Spanish in 1565. The Spanish started a mission for the Timucuas and lived on Amelia until they were defeated in the French and Indian War in 1763. England then took possession of Florida and flew the British flag. At the end of the Revolutionary War, in 1763, Florida was returned to Spain and the Spanish flag was again raised over Amelia.

At this point the Spanish built Fort San Carlos near the northern end of Amelia Island and developed a small town named Fernandina, named in honor of Spain's King Ferdinand VII, now referred to as Old Town. Because Amelia was not part of the U.S.A., but was directly across the river from Georgia, there were great opportunities for pirates and illegal trade from Florida into the U.S.A. No one had very much control during that time. Then in 1812 a plan was devised for the United States to take over East Florida. The Patriots of Florida in their gunboats moved toward the Spanish Fort San Carlos on Amelia Island. The Spanish incorrectly believed that the Patriots were ready to fire and they surrendered without a shot. The Patriot flag was raised. The very next day, the Patriots gave Amelia Island to the United Sates

Amelia Island is the only American soil that has been under eight different flags.

and the American flag was raised. Amelia was returned to the Spanish in several weeks to avoid confrontation.

Then in 1817 a group of con men from Darien, Georgia, with Gregor MacGregor in charge, raised the Green Cross of Florida flag. MacGregor left when he realized he was not able to stay in control.

A few days later Luis Aury came to the island with 130 of his own soldiers and $60.000. The people were pleased to accept some of the money and they granted him military command. He then raised the Mexican Rebel flag, a flag he just happened to have on his ship from a previous adventure. These soldiers did not get along with the people on the island and much fighting ensued. The United States forced Aury to surrender the island and the Stars and Stripes were raised again on December 23, 1817.

Amelia was a part of the Florida Territory until Florida became the 27th state in 1845. Fort Clinch was built in 1847 but was never fully completed. It is an example of brick European styled forts built during this era to protect the United

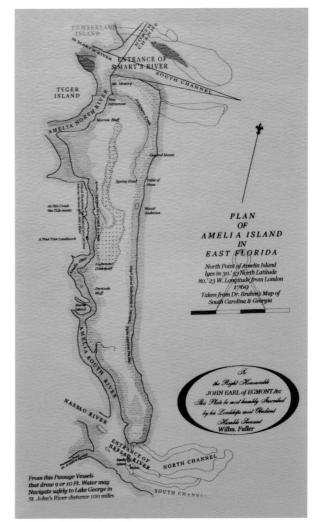

Historial chart of Amelia Island.

Yulee Railroad intering port at the Turn of the century.

Above is the Amelia Island Museum of History In the old jail house.

States, but as in most cases, no shots were ever fired. Florida seceded from the union in 1862 and the Confederate flag, the 8th, was flown for a short time, followed by the permanent United States flag. The original town of Fernandina was moved from Old Town to the area it is today to take advantage of the deep harbor for boat docking and easy access to the railroad. Because of the Yulee railroad, created by David Yulee, the Golden Era was a busy time of growth and wealth during the end of the 19th century.

Amelia's economy was slow during the first part of the 20th century, but regained much of its strength because of the shrimp industry, the paper mills and tourism. They have all worked together to stabilize the economy of this very special barrier island, filled with treasures of rich history and the beauty of nature.

We recommend reading more about the history of Amelia Island. Visit one of the Nassau County libraries, the Amelia Island Museum of History or the book and gift stores on the island.

Nassau County Historic Court House on Centre Street.

Today Amelia Island and Fernandina Beach are brimming with things to see and do. At the west end of Centre Street is the Fernandina Beach Marina where transient and local boats are docked.

Within a block or two are many restaurants and retail stores, from shoes and jewelry to shirts and books. There is even a wonderful homemade fudge shop. The old railroad building on Centre Street next to the railroad tracks is now the local Welcome Center and the Amelia Island Museum of History on 3rd Street is a must for learning more about the history of this area. The horse and buggy tours can take you to the historic buildings, such as the old courthouse and the many historic homes and churches that were built during the Golden Age around the late 1800's.

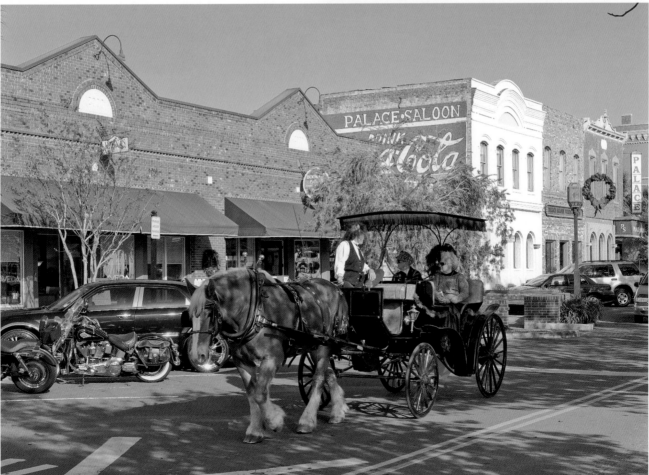

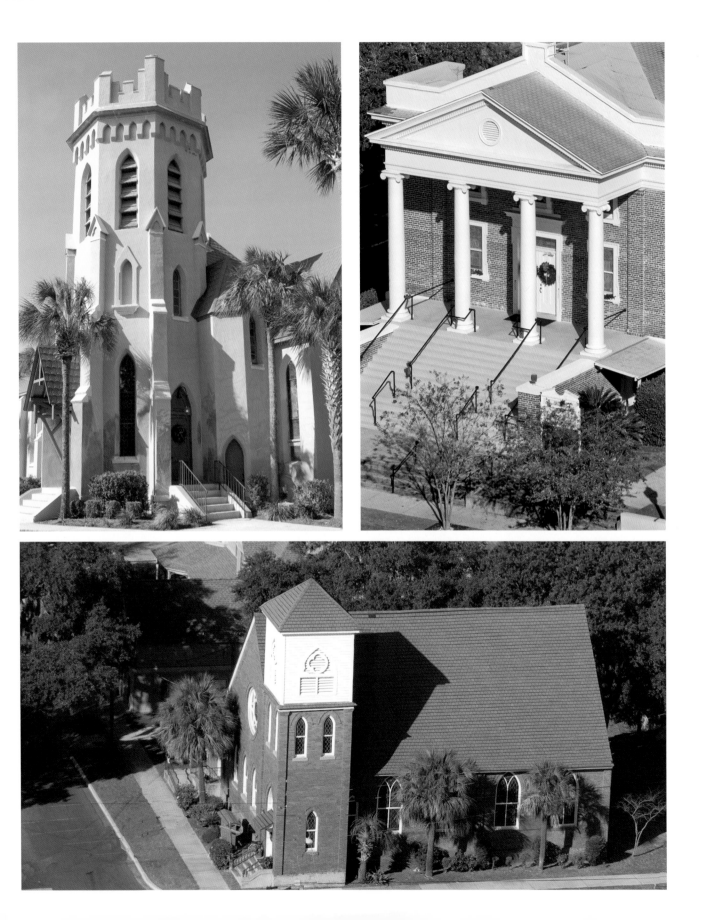

Along the Amelia River north of Fernandina you will see shrimp boats belonging to local shrimpers, many who have been in the area for several generations.

Next is the Port of Fernandina where large cargo ships arrive and depart regularly with merchandise from around the world. These large ships come from the Atlantic at the north end of Amelia Island because of the deep water in the Cumberland Sound.

After the paper mill is Old Town Fernandina and Plaza San Carlos. The movie "Pippi Longstocking" was filmed here and her home was the Captain's House on the parade ground square.

The entrance to Egan's Creek is next. There are several marinas here. Egan's Creek is a special place to see birds, alligators and other natural wildlife.

First constructed in 1820, the Amelia Island Lighthouse began its days on Cumberland Island, the southern most of Georgia's islands. The Light-house was moved to Amelia Island, where the light would better serve the navigational needs of the area. Under the National Historic Lighthouse Preservation Act of 2000, the Amelia Island Lighthouse was declared surplus and offered to Fernandina Beach.

Egan's Creek consists of over 300 acres of protected lands.

North end of Amelia Island on the Cumberland Sound.

Fort Clinch State Park is at the north end of Amelia Island. On the first weekend of every month there is a very entertaining enactment of what was happening at Fort Clinch in the mid 1800's. The doctor, seamstress, cook, musicians and soldiers all wear authentic costumes from that era.

The paths in the park are great for walk-ing or biking, the beach is beautiful and the view of Cumberland Island, Georgia across the Cumberland Sound is always interesting.

The two campgrounds here are usually quite busy. On the Atlantic Ocean side of Fort Clinch State Park is a long fishing pier also enjoyed by many people.

Amelia Island is 13 miles from north to south and 2 miles wide. Looking at the pristine beach it is possible to imagine how many people enjoy the sandy beach, watching the waves crash on the shore, playing and swimming in the water, building sand castles and images from the sand, hunting for special sea shells and shark's teeth,

fishing, biking, surfing, watching the birds or just relaxing. Private homes, hotels, bed and break-fast accommodations, resorts and many public access areas and parks are along the strand. The beach is for everyone!!!

American Beach was founded in 1935 as a vacation haven on the Atlantic beachfront for African-Americans. In January, 2002, after much diligent work by MaVynee Betsch, known as the Beach Lady, and many others, it was placed on the National Register of Historic Places. The Franklintown Church and parks are used for many activities.

A DUNE SYSTEM CALLED "NANA"

Located in American Beach on Amelia Island "Nana," at 60-foot, is the tallest sand dune system in the state of Florida. 10-acres is now preserved as a national park, part of the Timucuan Ecological and Historic Preserve and is designated as a "Florida Heritage Site," thanks to the efforts of the late MaVynne Betsch, known as "the Beach Lady." She felt ... "living peacefully in harmony with nature is the most rewarding lifestyle."

At the south end of the island is the Kelly Sea Horse Ranch. Learn about their scenic horse riding tours at www.kellyranchinc.com. The Amelia Island State Park and the twin bridges across to the Talbot State Parks and Jacksonville, Florida are at the tip of the island. Fishing from the old bridge and the beaches is a favorite activity for many people.

On the right after crossing the bridge to Big Talbot Island is Kayak Amelia. Here there is a wonderful opportunity to explore the rivers and marshes in a kayak with a guide on Simpson Creek, Fort George River and beyond. You might see dolphins, manatees, sea turtles and usually beautiful birds. Check their schedule at www.kayakamelia.com. Big Talbot is a quiet, beautiful destination on the beach.

Little Talbot State Park also has special beaches and a pleasant walking trail.

Big Talbot Island

Little Talbot Island

A little further south is Heugenot Island, where driving on the beach is allowed, and St. George Island where there is a fascinating old cotton plantation called Kingsley Plantation that can be explored and enjoyed. At the Ribault Club is an opportunity to take a tour with the Eco-motion Segway Tours. Go to www.ecomotiontours.com for more details.

Ribault Club

Kingsley Plantation

Our circumnavigation tour of Amelia Island is complete upon returning to the island and continuing up the Intracoastal Waterway along the marsh back past the airport and then to the Shave Bridge. The marsh is quiet and rich with wildlife. The sunsets can be phenomenal.

There are many interesting and pleasant things to do all over Amelia Island. It is fun to try various restaurants and browse in the very diverse shops all over the island. The Farmer's Market every Saturday morning is always special. Many annual events such as the Jazz Festival, the Concourse D'Elegance (an antique car exhibit) and the Shrimp Festival are enjoyed every year. Plus businesses are always thinking of pleasant ways to attract people, often including live music.

There are many local and transient boaters at the marinas and always fisherman on shore and in fishing boats. Many segments of the community are routinely busy with events for children.

Weddings and family gatherings occur regularly. There are several public and private golf courses on the island. Amelia River Cruises located at the Fernandina Beach Marina at the west end of Centre Street has a wonderful selection of tours every day.

Three of the favorites are the boat trip to and from St. Marys, Georgia, the tour to Cumberland Island and the excursion up Egan's Creek. The visual arts groups and the performing arts groups are both excellent and very active in the community with many planned events.

Appreciate and Enjoy all the Wonders of
Amelia Island and *Fernandina Beach.*